OPTIMISM

Reagan Miller

www.av2books.com

Step 1
Go to **www.av2books.com**

Step 2
Enter this unique code
CSQPWBX7S

Step 3
Explore your interactive eBook!

AV2 is optimized for use on any device

Your interactive eBook comes with...

Contents
Browse a live contents page to easily navigate through resources

Audio
Listen to sections of the book read aloud

Videos
Watch informative video clips

Weblinks
Gain additional information for research

Try This!
Complete activities and hands-on experiments

Key Words
Study vocabulary, and complete a matching word activity

Quizzes
Test your knowledge

Slideshows
View images and captions

... and much, much more!

OPTIMISM

Contents

What Is Optimism?

Optimism describes a positive attitude, or way of feeling or thinking about something or someone.

A person who has optimism is called an **optimist**. Optimists are hopeful that the situations they face will go well. They expect the best in the future and work hard to reach their **goals**. When faced with a problem or challenge, optimists focus on what they can do to improve the situation. They believe things will get better.

A person with a **negative** attitude is called a **pessimist**. When faced with a problem, pessimists are more likely to focus on what is wrong or unfair. They often feel helpless and unable to solve problems. They do not believe things will improve.

Optimism is not something people are born with or without. Everyone can learn to have a positive attitude. Just like learning anything new, it takes work and practice.

Why Is Optimism Important?

Optimism is important because it helps you get past challenges and keep reaching for your goals.

Imagine you tried out for the school soccer team. You worked hard, had fun, and even learned some new skills. When the coach posts the list of the kids who made the team, your name is not on it. How would you react to this situation?

A You decide that you are terrible at all sports and tell yourself you will never try out for any team again, ever.

B You ask a friend who made the team to help you with your soccer skills over the summer. You want to be ready to try out again next year.

It is normal to feel disappointed in this kind of situation. The difference between being a pessimist and being an optimist is how you respond or react to the situation.

Optimism is not just about hoping good things will happen. Optimists use positive thinking to make plans and take action to reach their goals, even when they feel disappointed about something.

Learn to Make Decisions

Which option best describes how an optimist would react to not making the team?

BIOGRAPHY

Khadijah Williams

Optimists believe a bright future is possible. They focus on what they can do to reach their goals rather than the challenges that may hold them back.

Khadijah Williams was homeless during most of her childhood. This means she and her family did not have a home to live in. Khadijah, her mother, and her younger sister lived in **shelters**, and sometimes had to sleep outside in parks. They moved around often in search of places to live. This caused Khadijah to miss a lot of school. She did not stay at one school for long. In fact, she went to 12 different schools in 12 years! Khadijah chose not to focus on the challenges she faced. Instead, she looked for lessons she could learn from her experiences.

NAME: **Khadijah Williams**
FROM: **Brooklyn, New York**
ACCOMPLISHMENT:
Overcame homelessness to earn top grades and a scholarship to Harvard University

Khadijah explains, "even though I could not really control where I would live or anything, I could control how much I wanted to learn." Her hard work and positive attitude helped her earn a scholarship to Harvard University, one of the top universities in the world! She has since graduated and continues to reach for new goals and focus on her bright future.

"To any person who does not like the situation they are in, and feels like they cannot do anything about it, they can...for a while, that is all I had—the belief that I could do it. All you need is that belief because you can. I did it."

—Khadijah Williams

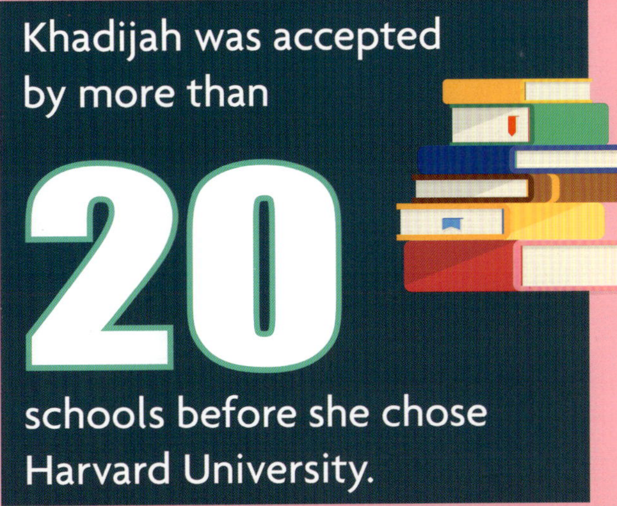

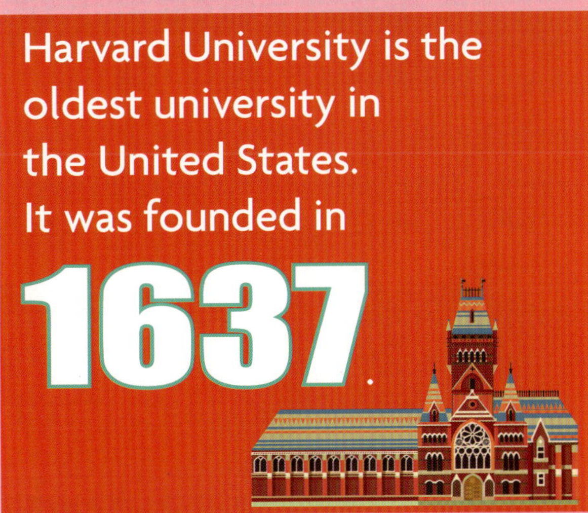

Optimism at Home

Self-talk describes the thoughts we have about ourselves and the situations we face. Self-talk can be negative or positive. A quiet place at home is a good place to practice self-talk.

Your thoughts are powerful! They affect your actions. Having negative thoughts about yourself or situations you face will make you feel less hopeful. You will be less likely to try to change or improve things. The good news is that you can change your self-talk from negative to positive.

1. Find a quiet place and pay attention to your self-talk. Are your thoughts positive and hopeful, or are they negative and discouraging? Are you being a friend to yourself, or a bully?

2. When you catch yourself using negative self-talk, stop and think about how you can change your thoughts to make them more positive.

Situation	Negative Self-Talk	Positive Self-Talk
You and your sister argue about what to watch on TV.	"We always fight! We will never get along!"	"It is normal for sisters to argue sometimes. If we calm down and listen to each other, I am sure we can figure this out."
You fall off your skateboard while learning a new trick.	"I will never get this right! Why am I so clumsy?"	"Even the pros take time to learn new tricks. I will keep trying."
You ask your brother and his friends to play, and they say no.	"Everyone hates me. I have no friends."	

Learn to Make Decisions

Read the third situation above. Complete the chart by changing the negative self-talk to positive.

Using words like "always," "never," and "everyone" can make a problem seem bigger than it is.

Optimism at School

A poor mark on a spelling quiz, not doing well on a class presentation, or losing a game in gym class are all examples of setbacks. It is normal to feel upset when you face them.

When you feel upset, it is what you do that matters most. Optimistic people look for ways to turn setbacks into successes! They think about what they can learn from their mistakes to improve in the future. Positive thinking inspires people to feel hopeful and keep trying when learning something new and challenging.

Optimistic people believe that setbacks are **temporary**, which means that they will not last. They believe they can improve with hard work.

When you face a setback, try to keep your mind open to different **solutions**. Talking with teachers, parents, and friends can be helpful. For example, you might ask your teacher for extra spelling work before your next quiz. You could make up spelling games with your friends to help all of you study.

Learn to Make Decisions

Think about a setback you faced at school. How did you find a solution?

Optimism in Your Community

A community is a group of people who live, work, and play in a place. Your home, school, and neighborhood are part of your community.

Optimists are more likely to try new things, such as getting involved with community events and groups. This is because optimists have **confidence**. When people are confident, they believe in themselves and expect they will be successful when they work hard. People who are not confident often avoid trying new things because they expect to fail before they even try.

Optimists try new things and face challenges with an attitude of "I can" instead of "I cannot."

Optimists look for ways to improve and grow. They do not compare themselves to others and are not afraid of making mistakes. Optimists know that everyone makes mistakes when trying something new. Getting involved in new activities is a way to make new friends who share your interests. What kinds of groups or clubs are available in your community? Find one that meets your interests. Ask a parent or adult to help you learn more about joining!

Joining a group or club in your community can help you discover that you are capable of more than you thought you were!

BIOGRAPHY

Robby Novak

Having a positive attitude can make a big difference in your life and in the lives of the people around you! Robby Novak is a great example of how one person's positive attitude can encourage others. Robby Novak may be better known as "Kid President."

Since 2012, Robby and his brother-in-law, Brad Montague, have made videos and shared them online. In the videos, Robby as "Kid President" encourages kids and grown-ups to work together to solve problems and make the world a better place. He tells people to celebrate the good things around them. Robby's goal is to "make the world more awesome!" Millions of people have seen Robby's videos. His positive message has spread around the world. Robby was born with a **condition** that makes his bones weak.

NAME: **Robby Novak**
FROM: **Henderson, Tennessee**
ACCOMPLISHMENT:
As "Kid President," Robby encourages people to work together to make the world a better place.

Learn to Make Decisions

Robby wants people to make the world more awesome. What positive message could you share with others?

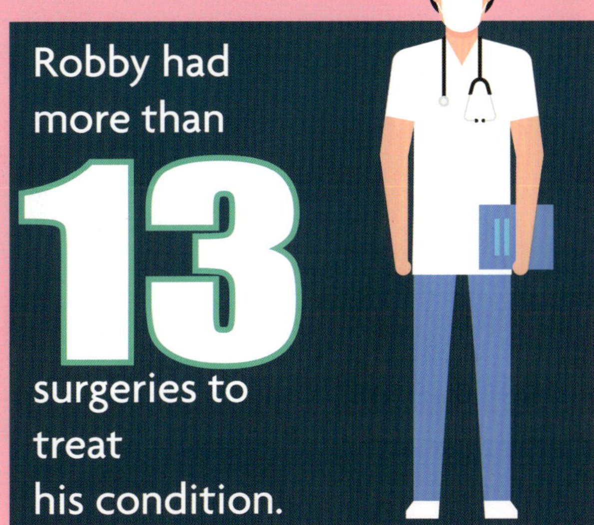

Robby has had more than 70 broken bones. He does not let his condition hold him back. He focuses on sharing his positive attitude (and dance moves!) with others.

"You just need to remember: You were born for a reason and you have a purpose, to be awesome and to do awesome things. And you are more capable than you know."

—Robby Novak

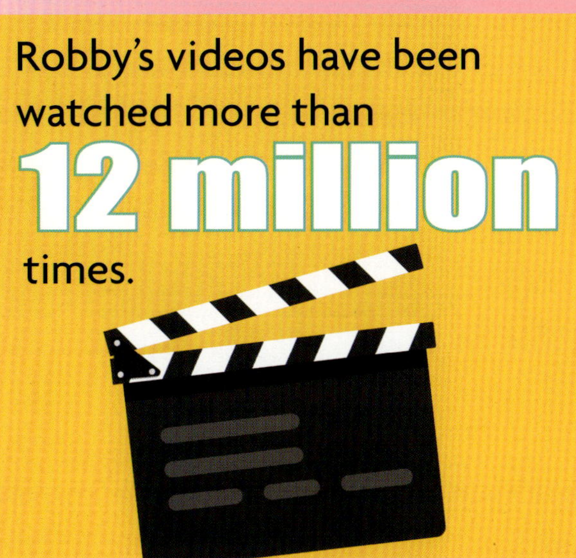

Forward Thinking

Everyone faces challenges and problems. Sometimes you cannot control the things that happen in your life. One thing you can always control, however, is how you react or respond to the things that happen.

You can always choose to have a positive attitude. By focusing on what you can do to make a situation better, you will feel more in control. Here are some **strategies** that can help you stay positive during challenging times:

Do not let negative things that have happened in the past stop you from trying something today. Focus on what you can do today to be successful in the future.

Think about times when you you have overcome challenges. These thoughts can help you feel hopeful. They may also give you ideas for how you can overcome a current challenge.

Focus on what is positive in a situation rather than what is negative.

Optimists believe they have the power to move their lives in positive directions.

"Life is 10 percent what happens to you and 90 percent how you react to it."

—Charles R. Swindoll, writer and speaker

Learn to Make Decisions

What could you say to a friend who wanted to give up on a goal?

Promote Positivity

A role model is someone who acts in a way that sets a good example for others.

Khadijah Williams and Robby Novak are role models who encourage others to live with optimism. You can be a role model to others by showing your positive attitude and sharing what you have learned in this book.

Here are some ways you can promote positivity!

Encourage friends and family to look at setbacks as chances to learn and improve.

Be just as excited about the success of others as you are about your own.

Share stories about positive people and events you hear about in your community and around the world.

Share what you learned about self-talk to help others change their thoughts from negative to positive.

Remind people of their past successes and other times when they have overcome setbacks.

Stepping Forward

Optimism is something you will continue to work on and improve throughout your life. Use the statements below to help you learn about your level of optimism. Use your results to help you find ways you can improve your optimism. There are no right or wrong anwers. Use this page again and again in the future to help make sure you keep stepping forward with optimism!

Read each statement. How well does it describe you? Think about your recent thoughts and actions to help you decide.

Key Words

condition: a state of health
confidence: belief in one's abilities to succeed through hard work
goals: objectives that you are trying to achieve
negative: describing the bad qualities of someone or something
optimist: a person who has optimism, or a positive attitude
pessimist: a person who has a negative attitude, or sees the worst in things
positive: describing something with an agreeable or favorable effect
scholarship: money or aid given to students to help them go to school, usually earned by accomplishments such as high grades
self-talk: the thoughts and words we tell ourselves
setbacks: challenges or stops to progress
shelters: buildings that can be used as a temporary home for people who are homeless
solutions: methods or ways of solving a problem
strategies: plans for achieving a goal
temporary: describing something that is not permanent or does not last long

Index

Get the best of both worlds.

AV2 bridges the gap between print and digital.

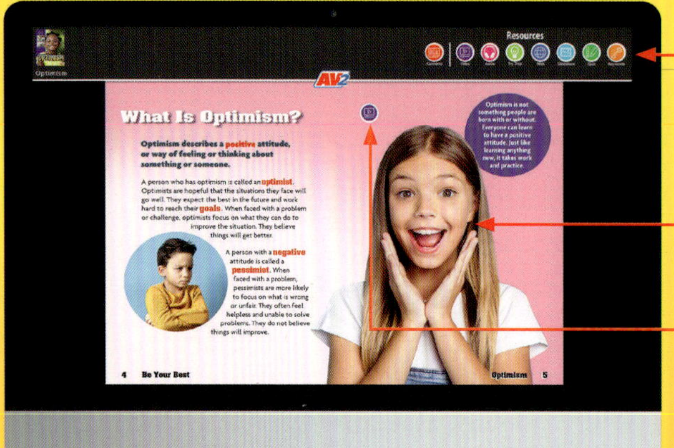

The expandable resources toolbar enables quick access to content including **videos**, **audio**, **activities**, **weblinks**, **slideshows**, **quizzes**, and **key words**.

Animated videos make static images come alive.

Resource icons on each page help readers to further **explore key concepts**.

Published by AV2
350 5th Avenue, 59th Floor
New York, NY, 10118
Website: www.av2books.com

Library of Congress Control Number: 2020937071

ISBN 978-1-7911-2795-4 (Hardcover)
ISBN 978-1-7911-2796-1 (Softcover)
ISBN 978-1-7911-2797-8 (Multi-user eBook)
ISBN 978-1-7911-2798-5 (Single-user eBook)

Printed in Guangzhou, China
1 2 3 4 5 6 7 8 9 0 24 23 22 21 20

042020
101119

Project Coordinator: Sara Cucini Designer: Jean Faye Marie Rodriguez

Every reasonable effort has been made to trace ownership and to obtain permission to reprint copyright material. The publishers would be pleased to have any errors or omissions brought to their attention so that they may be corrected in subsequent printings.

The publisher acknowledges iStock, Getty Images, and Shutterstock as its primary image suppliers for this title.

First published by Crabtree Publishing Company in2017.